OCEAN LIFE UP CLOSE

Octopuses

by Christina Leaf

BELLWETHER MEDIA · MINNEAPOLIS, MN

Note to Librarians, Teachers, and Parents:

Blastoff! Readers are carefully developed by literacy experts and combine standards-based content with developmentally appropriate text.

Level 1 provides the most support through repetition of high-frequency words, light text, predictable sentence patterns, and strong visual support.

Level 2 offers early readers a bit more challenge through varied simple sentences, increased text load, and less repetition of high-frequency words.

Level 3 advances early-fluent readers toward fluency through increased text and concept load, less reliance on visuals, longer sentences, and more literary language.

Level 4 builds reading stamina by providing more text per page, increased use of punctuation, greater variation in sentence patterns, and increasingly challenging vocabulary.

Level 5 encourages children to move from "learning to read" to "reading to learn" by providing even more text, varied writing styles, and less familiar topics.

Whichever book is right for your reader, Blastoff! Readers are the perfect books to build confidence and encourage a love of reading that will last a lifetime!

This edition first published in 2017 by Bellwether Media, Inc.

No part of this publication may be reproduced in whole or in part without written permission of the publisher. For information regarding permission, write to Bellwether Media, Inc., Attention: Permissions Department, 5357 Penn Avenue South, Minneapolis, MN 55419.

Library of Congress Cataloging-in-Publication Data

Names: Leaf, Christina, author.
Title: Octopuses / by Christina Leaf.
Description: Minneapolis, MN : Bellwether Media, Inc., [2017] | Series:
    Blastoff! Readers. Ocean Life Up Close | Audience: Ages 5-8. | Audience: K to
    grade 3. | Includes bibliographical references and index.
Identifiers: LCCN 2015048070 | ISBN 9781626174191 (hardcover : alk. paper)
Subjects: LCSH: Octopuses–Juvenile literature.
Classification: LCC QL430.3.O2 L43 2017 | DDC 594.56–dc23
LC record available at http://lccn.loc.gov/2015048070

Printed in the United States of America, North Mankato, MN.

Table of Contents

What Are Octopuses?

Octopuses are **cephalopods** known for their eight arms. They are among the world's smartest creatures!

Other Cephalopods

cuttlefish

nautiluses

squids

These **invertebrates** are fast learners. They can solve problems and use tools for tasks.

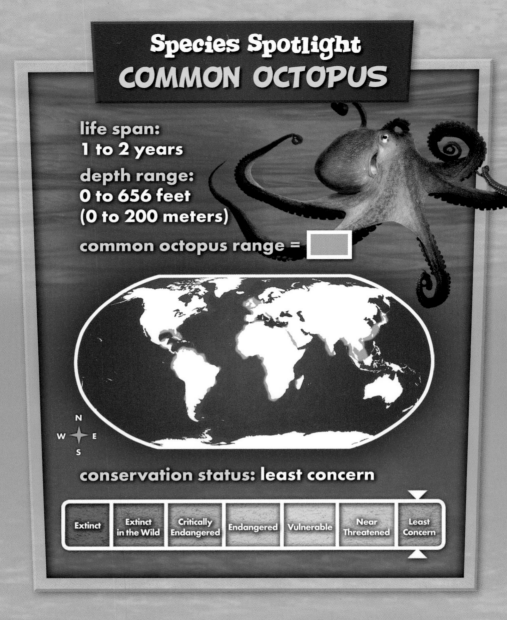

COMMON OCTOPUS

life span:
1 to 2 years

depth range:
**0 to 656 feet
(0 to 200 meters)**

common octopus range =

conservation status: **least concern**

Extinct	Extinct in the Wild	Critically Endangered	Endangered	Vulnerable	Near Threatened	Least Concern

Many octopuses prefer shallow coasts. Some live deep below the water's surface.

Most octopuses live in dens. They make homes in **coral reefs** or rocky areas.

day
octopus

Well Armed

Octopuses come in many sizes. Some are less than 1 inch (2.5 centimeters) long. The largest can stretch 30 feet (9 meters) from arm to arm!

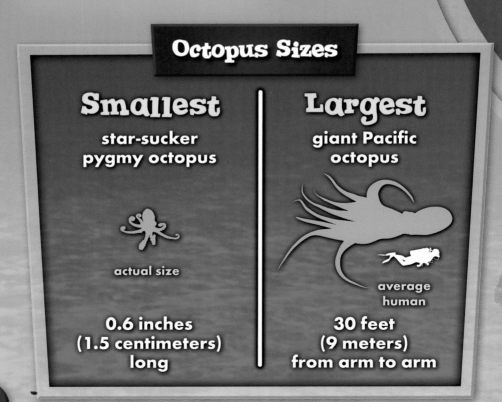

Octopus Sizes

Smallest
star-sucker pygmy octopus

actual size

0.6 inches
(1.5 centimeters)
long

Largest
giant Pacific octopus

average human

30 feet
(9 meters)
from arm to arm

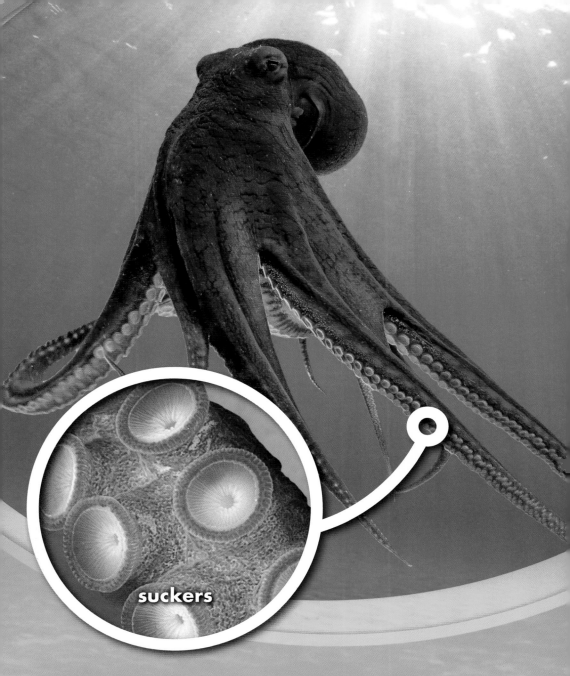

suckers

The long arms sit below the
head. **Suckers** line each arm.

An octopus's body is soft and muscular. A bag-like **mantle** on top of the head holds and protects its **organs**.

mantle

Identify an Octopus

eight arms

large eyes

rounded body

Two large eyes give the octopus excellent eyesight. They are on either side of the head.

Sneak Attackers

Most octopuses hunt at night. These **carnivores** sneak up on **prey**. They eat lobsters, crabs, and other **crustaceans**.

Mussels and small fish are other favorite foods. Sometimes, octopuses eat other octopuses.

Catch of the Day

bogues

green crabs

great scallops

Octopuses hold meals with the suckers on their arms. Some use **venom** to slow prey down.

common
octopus

beak

A hard beak beneath the body cracks the shells of prey. Then octopuses use empty shells to decorate! They scatter them outside their dens.

Amazing Escapes

coconut octopus

Octopuses move with their arms. Usually, they crawl along the ocean floor. Some octopuses walk on two arms.

At times, they force water through their mantles to shoot backward. But this takes a lot of energy.

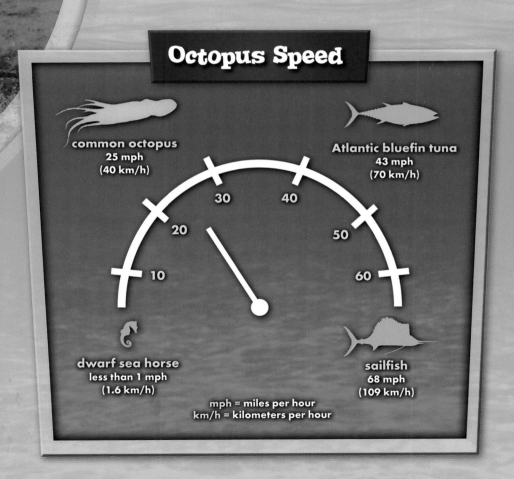

Octopus Speed

common octopus
25 mph
(40 km/h)

Atlantic bluefin tuna
43 mph
(70 km/h)

30   40

20   50

10   60

dwarf sea horse
less than 1 mph
(1.6 km/h)

sailfish
68 mph
(109 km/h)

mph = miles per hour
km/h = kilometers per hour

Many **predators** hunt octopuses. To stay safe, octopuses hide. Their boneless bodies squeeze into small spaces.

They are also masters of **camouflage**. Octopuses can change their skin to match colors, patterns, and even **textures**!

Sea Enemies

whitetip reef sharks

great barracudas

harbor seals

When predators get close, octopuses may squirt a cloud of ink. This hides them, so they can jet away quickly.

An octopus may lose
an arm in its escape.
But it can grow a
new one!

Glossary

camouflage—a way of using color to blend in with surroundings

carnivores—animals that only eat meat

cephalopods—animals that have excellent eyesight, ink sacs, and muscular arms with suckers; cuttlefish, octopuses, and squids are types of cephalopods.

coral reefs—structures made of coral that usually grow in shallow seawater

crustaceans—animals that have several pairs of legs and hard outer shells; crabs and lobsters are types of crustaceans.

invertebrates—animals without a backbone

mantle—a fold of thick skin that keeps an octopus's body safe

organs—parts of a body with certain jobs

predators—animals that hunt other animals for food

prey—animals that are hunted by other animals for food

suckers—body parts that suck or cling; octopuses also use their suckers to taste.

textures—ways in which things look and feel

venom—a poison an octopus makes

To Learn More

AT THE LIBRARY

Gray, Leon. *Giant Pacific Octopus: The World's Largest Octopus*. New York, N.Y.: Bearport Publishing, 2013.

Olsen, Alana. *Look Out for the Blue-Ringed Octopus!* New York, N.Y.: PowerKids Press, 2016.

Shea, Therese. *The Bizarre Life Cycle of an Octopus*. New York, N.Y.: Gareth Stevens Pub., 2013.

ON THE WEB

Learning more about octopuses is as easy as 1, 2, 3.

1. Go to www.factsurfer.com.

2. Enter "octopuses" into the search box.

3. Click the "Surf" button and you will see a list of related web sites.

With factsurfer.com, finding more information is just a click away.

Index